SUPER SLUMBER PARTIES

By Brooks Whitney

Illustrated by Nadine Bernard Westcott

Published by Pleasant Company Publications
© 1997 by Pleasant Company

Printed in the United States of America.
    99 00 01 WCR 10 9 8 7 6

American Girl Library® is a registered trademark of
Pleasant Company.

Editorial Development: Andrea Weiss
Art Direction: Kym Abrams
Design: Annette Smaga, Ingrid Hess, Holly Puff
Recipe Concepts, pages 15 and 16: Marlene Goldsmith

Library of Congress Cataloging-in-Publication Data
Whitney, Brooks.
Super slumber parties / by Brooks Whitney ;
illustrated by Nadine Westcott.
     p.   cm
"American girl library."
Summary: Creative ideas for games, crafts, food, decorations,
and favors, as well as planning and trouble-shooting tips,
to guarantee a successful sleepover.
ISBN 1-56247-529-0
1. Sleepovers—Juvenile literature. 2. Children's
parties—Juvenile literature. [1. Sleepovers. 2. Parties.]
I. Westcott, Nadine Bernard, ill. II. American girl (Middleton,
Wis.) III. Title.
GV1205.W55   1997 793.2'1—dc21   97-12894 CIP AC

AmericanGirl Library®

SUPER SLUMBER PARTIES

By Brooks Whitney

Illustrated by Nadine Bernard Westcott

PLEASANT COMPANY PUBLICATIONS™

Contents

Dream Up a Theme

10 Secrets to a

What's the key to a successful sleepover? *Think ahead!* Remember these top ten tips and you're guaranteed a good time for everyone.

1 Keep It Small

Don't invite too many people. The more guests you have, the harder it is to control things. Most girls recommend limiting the guest list to four or five friends who get along well with one another.

2 No Surprises!

Discuss the rules of the party with your parents beforehand. Decide which rooms are off-limits, what time lights-out will be, and what kind of privacy you will have from your parents and other family members.

3 Make a Game Plan

Discuss ideas for activities, food, and decorations with your parents. Be sure to plan at least three big activities. Don't try to wing it the night of the party by thinking up activities as you go—guests get grumpy when there's a lull in the action.

4 Write It Down

Make a list of everything you are planning to do and serve at the party. Then write down exactly what you will need for each of those things.

5 Be Resourceful

A great party doesn't have to cost a lot! Use materials from around the house to make your own decorations, invitations, prizes, and favors.

Important! Whenever you see this symbol next to instructions in this book, it means you'll need an adult's help.

Super Sleepover

6 Testing, 1-2-3

If you plan to use any equipment, such as a VCR, CD player, or computer, make sure it's working properly and that you know exactly how to operate it.

8 Light the Way

Put a night-light in the bathroom, and keep hallways lit. When your friends first arrive, give them a tour of the house so they know where things are.

9 Play Fair

Avoid rowdy games such as pillow fights, games that cause embarrassment such as Truth or Dare, and other activities that could lead to injuries or hurt feelings.

7 Get the Scoop

Check with each guest to see if she has any health needs or preferences that may require special arrangements. Does she have any allergies? Is she a vegetarian?

10 Say Good Night

Have a separate "snooze room" where girls who want to go to sleep earlier can lay out their sleeping bags when they first arrive. As the night goes on, sleepy girls can go to bed while night owls stay up and play.

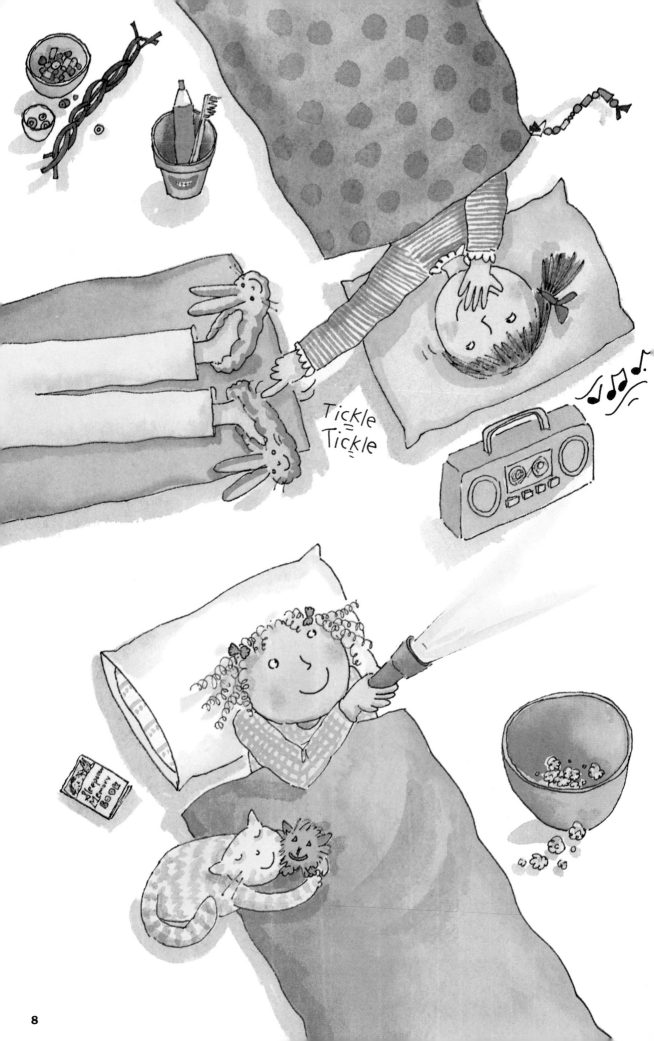

Tickle
Tickle

Party Time!

Invite your friends to join you for an evening of silly games, super snacks, sleeping bag fun, and special times. Then celebrate your friendship into the night.

Eye-Opening Invitations

Be an overnight sensation with these attention-getting invitations!

Flash Cards

Pass out mini flashlights with invitations hidden in the battery compartments!

You will need:

- Construction paper or notepaper
- Pens or markers
- Scissors
- Yarn or ribbon
- Mini flashlights, 1 for each guest

1 Write the party information on a slip of paper and poke a hole in one corner. Then tie one end of a 4-inch piece of yarn or ribbon through the hole.

> Come to a Sleepover!
> Where: Ingrid's house
> 1538 Oak Drive
> When: Friday, April 22
> 7:30 P.M.
> Pickup Time: 9:30 A.M. Saturday

2 Remove the batteries from the flashlight. Tuck the paper into the battery compartment with the ribbon hanging out, and put the top back on.

3 Cut out a small moon- or star-shaped piece of paper. Write "Surprise Inside . . ." and tie it to the other end of the ribbon.

> Come to a Sleepover!
> Where: Kim's house
> 123 Elm St.
> When: Sat, Aug. 6
> 7:30 P.M.

> Breakfast at 8:00 A.M.
> Good-byes at 9:00 A.M.

Night and Day

Use a glue stick to glue a sheet of black construction paper and a sheet of blue construction paper back to back. With a pencil, trace on the paper around the outside of a bowl or plate. Cut out the circle. Use silver glitter and glue to make a crescent moon on the black side. Use a silver pen or crayon to write where and when the party starts. Decorate with star stickers. Let dry overnight.

The next day, use gold glitter and glue to decorate the blue side with a cheery sun, and use a gold pen or crayon to write when the party ends.

Sweet Dreams

This clever card won't be a yawn!

You will need:
- 8½-by-11-inch sheet of paper, one for each guest
- Ruler
- Pencil
- Scissors
- Markers or crayons

1 Fold the paper in half lengthwise. With the ruler, measure 3 inches down from the top along the outside edge of the paper. Mark the spot with pencil.

2 Starting at the mark, cut straight across the top layer of paper to the crease. Then cut all the way up the crease. Discard the cutout piece.

3 Decorate the front of the card to look like a sleeping bag. On the inside draw a sleeping girl so that her head shows when you close the card. Write the party information on the left side.

You're invited to spend the night!
Time: 7:00 P.M.
Saturday, June 7
Place: Ann's house
18 Baker St.
Pickup Time: 9:30 A.M.
Sunday
Bring a sleeping bag and a pillow.

Something to Smile About

Use puff paints or permanent markers to decorate a toothbrush for each of your guests. Then write the party information on colored paper, punch a hole in one corner of the paper, and use a ribbon to tie the paper to the neck of the toothbrush.

Party Tips

- List on the invitation anything special that you want your guests to bring, such as flashlights, stuffed animals, or supplies needed for a particular craft or game.
- To avoid hurt feelings, never pass out invitations in front of girls who aren't invited to your party.

11

Create Your Own Space

Transform your sleeping space into the perfect party place with fluffy pillows, magical lighting, and other special touches.

Night-Lights

Special lighting will add a cozy glow to any party room. Ask an adult to help you replace the lightbulbs in the lamps and fixtures with colored bulbs. Or hang twinkly holiday lights around the door frames and windows of the party room.

Box of Fun

It's always a good idea to have a supply of icebreakers and boredom busters on hand. Fill a big box or basket with fun things to play with, such as yo-yos, paddle balls, jacks, playing cards, Slinkies, and string for Cat's Cradle.

Streamer Tent

Have an adult help you attach brightly colored streamers to the center of the ceiling with masking tape. Then gently pull the streamers out to the sides, twisting as you go, to form a tepee shape. Hold the ends down with books or other heavy objects.

Pillow Pile

To create a comfy place to lounge, collect pillows from around the house and pile them into a big squishy mound. Add stuffed animals for cuddly companions.

Doodle here!

Doodle Sheet

Use masking tape to hang a big sheet of paper on the wall, or spread the paper out across the floor or over a table. Have a supply of markers, crayons, stickers, and stamps on hand to doodle with throughout the evening. By morning, you'll have a great party souvenir!

Party Tips

- Make sure you clear enough space for all your guests to roll out their sleeping bags.
- Remove any breakable objects from the party room.

The Main Course

Serve an assortment of fun foods to satisfy everyone's cravings.

Tiny Dining

Prepare a feast fit for a fairy princess! Serve a buffet of these tiny foods.

Mini Munchies

Cherry tomatoes, baby carrots, bite-size crackers, and miniature boxes of raisins make fun snacks.

Doll-Size Deli

Serve sandwiches on mini bagels, small party rye, or French bread rounds.

Piglets in a Blanket

Wrap mini hot dogs in ready-made crescent dough. Bake at 350 degrees for 5 to 10 minutes, or until golden brown.

Ice Cream Sandwichlets

Use a melon-ball scoop to spoon ice cream between bite-size cookies.

Sleeping Bag Roll-Ups

Give your guests a choice of fillings to create their own crescent roll sandwiches.

You will need:
- Ready-made crescent roll dough, such as Pillsbury
- Fillings, such as shredded cheese, thin slices of deli meat, peanut butter, jelly, and cream cheese.

1 Follow the directions on the package to separate the dough into triangles.

2 Have each guest place the fillings of her choice at the wide end of a triangle and roll the dough toward the point.

3 Have an adult help you place the crescent rolls on a cookie sheet and bake according to directions.

Pizza Parlor

Open your own pizzeria! Set out a variety of ingredients and let each guest invent an ooey, gooey, cheesy creation.

Pizza Picasso

Be pizza painters! Use bagels, English muffins, pita bread, or tortillas for crust "canvases," and provide an assortment of shredded cheeses and toppings to arrange in pretty patterns. For example, make a flower out of pepperoni petals and a green-pepper stem!

"Dough" It Yourself!

Create your own miniature deep-dish pizzas.

You will need:
- Ready-made pizza dough, such as Pillsbury
- Muffin tin
- Spoon and fork
- Sauce, shredded cheese, and an assortment of fillings
- Baking sheet

1 Have each guest press some dough into one of the muffin tin compartments.

2 Have your guests spoon sauce on their dough, sprinkle it with cheese, then top with the fillings of their choice.

3 With an adult's help, place the muffin tin on a baking sheet and bake at 350 degrees for 15 to 20 minutes. Pop the pizzas out with a fork.

Play with Your Food

These silly snacks are as much fun to make as they are to eat!

Tasty Trinkets

Nibble the night away on edible baubles and beads.

Licorice Bracelets

Licorice whip, or shoestring licorice, is perfect for braiding, knotting, and twisting.

Cereal Necklaces

Thread cereal such as Froot Loops or Cheerios onto pieces of string. Tie the crunchy creations around your neck for lip-smacking snacking.

Gummy Charm Bracelets

Use a needle and thread to string up charming bracelets of gummy treats to trade and taste.

Pretzel Designs

Form hearts, stars, your initials, or even short messages—then eat the evidence!

You will need:
- 2 cups white flour
- 1 tablespoon vegetable oil
- 1 tablespoon yeast
- ¾ cup lukewarm apple or orange juice
- Bowl
- Baking sheet
- Pastry brush or wax paper
- 1 beaten egg
- Salt

1 Mix the flour, oil, yeast, and juice in the bowl. Knead the dough by pushing and pulling hard with your hands for a few minutes. Add a little flour if the dough gets sticky.

2 Tear off small pieces of dough and roll them between your palms to make "snakes." Form the snakes into shapes.

3 Put the shapes on a lightly oiled baking sheet and let rise for 30 minutes. Preheat the oven to 450 degrees.

4 Lightly brush or smear the pretzel shapes with the egg. Then sprinkle them with salt. Have an adult help you bake the pretzels for 15 minutes, or until golden brown.

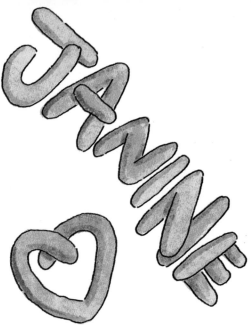

Rock 'n' Roll Ice Cream

Turn on the tunes and "rock and roll" a few ingredients into a cool dessert.

You will need:
- 2 clean coffee cans, a 13-ounce and a 2-pound size, each with a plastic lid
- 1 cup whole milk
- 1 cup heavy cream
- ½ cup sugar
- 1 teaspoon vanilla extract
- Optional add-ins, such as chocolate chips, strawberries, or banana slices
- 1 large bag crushed ice
- 2 cups rock salt
- Newspaper
- Mixing spoon
- Mittens or gloves

1 In the small coffee can, combine the milk, cream, sugar, vanilla, and add-in of your choice. Put the lid on.

2 Place the small can inside the big can. Pack the space between the 2 cans tightly with ice. Sprinkle 1 cup of rock salt over the ice. Put the lid on the big can.

3 Cover a table with newspaper. Roll the can back and forth over it for about 4 minutes or until the can starts to leak. Then take turns carefully shaking the can for another 4 to 5 minutes. Wear mittens or gloves if your hands get cold!

4 Open both cans. Dump out the ice and salt. Stir the ice cream. Pack with fresh ice and salt, then roll and shake for another 8 to 10 minutes. Be patient—it's worth the wait!

Midnight Munchies

Fruity Fizz

Pour different-flavored juices into ice cube trays and freeze for 3 to 4 hours, or until solid. Add the colorful cubes to Sprite, 7-Up, or ginger ale. For silly straws, snip the tips off licorice sticks and slurp away!

Snack Bar

Set out a variety of snacks, both sweet and salty, such as:

- popcorn
- dried fruit
- assorted nuts
- mini marshmallows
- granola and other cereals
- chocolate chips
- shredded coconut
- sunflower seeds
- mini crackers or cookies
- Milk Duds
- pretzels
- yogurt-covered raisins
- caramel squares

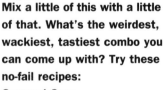

Mix a little of this with a little of that. What's the weirdest, wackiest, tastiest combo you can come up with? Try these no-fail recipes:

Caramel Corn
   Milk Duds + popcorn

Tropical Crunch
   Coconut + banana chips + cashews

S'mores
   Mini marshmallows + Teddy Grahams + chocolate chips

Taffy Apples
   Dried apple chips + caramels + peanuts

When it's time for a snack attack, satisfy your late night cravings with any of these delicious treats.

Chocolate Fun-due

Take a dreamy midnight dip in a bowl of melted chocolate!

You will need:

- 1 cup semisweet chocolate chips
- ½ cup evaporated milk
- ¼ cup mini marshmallows
- Microwave-safe bowl
- Forks, skewers, or long toothpicks
- Strawberries, banana slices, pineapple chunks, or pieces of pound cake

1 Combine the evaporated milk, chocolate chips, and marshmallows in the bowl.

2 Have an adult help you microwave on LOW for 2 minutes. Remove and stir. Microwave for 1 to 2 more minutes. Stir until smooth.

3 Use the forks, skewers, or toothpicks to dunk the fruit or cake into the chocolate sauce. Be careful—it's hot!

Freeze Until Midnight

Waiting is half the fun when everyone makes these frozen desserts together!

Candy Pops

Turn chewy candy bars into popsicles. Remove the wrappers, insert wooden sticks, and freeze for 2 hours.

Go Bananas!

Your buddies will go nutty for frozen bananas. Peel a banana and cut it in half. Insert a wooden stick into the cut end. Dip in chocolate sauce and roll in chopped nuts. Lay on wax paper and freeze for 2 hours.

Time for Beddy-Pie

Create mini ice cream pies by scooping softened ice cream into pre-made tart crusts. Spread chocolate or butterscotch sauce over the ice cream. Sprinkle chopped nuts or toffee on top. Freeze for 1 to 2 hours.

Clowning Around

What are sleepover parties for?
Late-night kookiness and giggles galore!

Double Trouble

Turn your usual bedtime routine into a comedy act with a few basic props and the help of a partner's arms.

You will need:
- **A big button-down shirt**
- **A small table**
- **A stool and a chair**
- **Props such as a toothbrush, hairbrush, and washcloth**

1 Place the stool behind the table, with the chair close behind the stool. Put the props on the table.

2 Sit on the stool with your hands clasped behind your back. Have another girl sit in the chair and slip her arms through yours.

3 Have someone help put the shirt over you, with the buttons toward the back and your partner's arms through the sleeves.

4 IT'S SHOWTIME! Describe your bedtime routine while your partner uses the props to act it out. It's harder—and funnier—than you think! Have everyone take turns trying.

Upside-Down Theater

Have two or more girls lie on their backs with their heads hanging off the end of a bed or couch. Lightly tie a scarf around the upper part of each girl's face so only the mouth and chin are showing. Using eyeliner, draw two eyes on the chin. Add a mustache for a man, or blush and lipstick for a woman. Have the upside-down girls act out a goofy skit, sing a duet, or tell jokes. The rest of you watching will hardly believe your eyes!

HA!

Have everyone lie on the floor in a circle with their heads on one another's stomachs. Going around the circle, have the first girl say, "Ha," the second girl say, "Ha-ha," the third say, "Ha-ha-ha," and so on. Before you know it, the combination of ha-has and jiggling stomachs will have everyone rolling with laughter.

Hairy Hairstyles

Have lots of fun hair supplies handy, such as barrettes, scrunchies, headbands, hair clips, brushes, and combs. Take turns creating the wackiest "do's" you can think of on each other. Then award prizes in different categories, such as Most Original or Scariest. For prizes, allow the winners to choose one or two hair accessories to take home.

Party Tips

Have a couple of disposable cameras handy for capturing those one-in-a-million moments.

Curl up in your bags with a hilarious video, such as:
- *The Princess Bride*
- *The Wrong Trousers*
- *The Pink Panther*

Games Galore

Plan some games that will get your guests scrambling, squirming, racing, and rolling!

Sleeping Bag Sports

You can't lose with these silly sack games!

Wiggle Worm

Make up an obstacle course of things to crawl around, over, and under—in your sleeping bags! Be sure to remove anything breakable. Then time yourselves wiggling through the course.

Who's Inside?

Choose one girl to leave the room while the rest of you hide in different sleeping bags. Then call the girl back into the room and have her try to guess who's in each bag by feeling through the material. Be sure not to giggle or you'll give yourselves away!

Musical Sleeping Bags

Choose a "disc jockey." Have everyone else arrange their sleeping bags in a circle, head to toe. Then remove one bag and close up the circle. Have the DJ play music while the rest of you walk around the bags. When the music stops, everyone must get into a bag. The girl left bagless is out. Remove a sleeping bag and continue playing until only one person is left.

Favorite Things

Find out how well you know one another. Give everyone a heart-shaped piece of paper and a pencil. Have each girl write on the heart her favorite color, movie, book, food, and animal without showing anybody else. Then put all the hearts into a pillowcase. Take turns drawing a heart and reading it out loud. Try to guess who is being described!

Stuffed Animal Races

You'll need a stuffed animal for every player. Create a starting line on one side of the room and a finish line on the other. In between, use shoes, socks, or pieces of paper to mark off 15 to 20 "spaces" on the floor. Line up the stuffed animals on the starting line. Then deal a playing card to each player. The players should move their animals the number of spaces shown on their cards. If a player draws a king, queen, or jack, her animal goes back to the start! Keep dealing until you have a winner.

On a Roll

Turn the party room into a life-size game board, with you as the pieces! First, have the group think of six different ways to walk, such as taking baby steps, hopping, etc. Write them down and number them 1 to 6. Then have everyone line up in one corner of the room. The first player rolls a pair of dice, one die at a time. The first die tells how many steps to take toward the next corner of the room. The second die tells what kind of steps to take. If the player rolls doubles, she must do the movement backward! The first girl to make it all the way around the room wins.

Party Tips

- Award prizes in lots of different categories and events to give everyone a chance to be a winner.
- Make sure you plan plenty of group games that don't require teams or partners. Competition can sometimes lead to fighting.

MOST TICKLISH

Craft Corner

Do projects with your pals to create super souvenirs—and special sleepover memories.

Sponge Stamp Sleep Shirts

These sleepy T's are guaranteed to please!

You will need:
- Sponges
- Scissors
- Newspaper and cardboard
- 1 large cotton T-shirt, such as a man's undershirt, for each guest
- Fabric paint
- Paper plates

1 Cut moon and star shapes out of the sponges.

2 Cover your work area with newspaper. Place cardboard or newspaper inside the T-shirts to keep the paint from soaking through.

3 Pour a small amount of paint onto a plate. Use a sponge to spread the paint into a thin layer.

4 Wet the sponge stamps slightly and squeeze them out. Then press them into the paint and onto the shirts. Rinse out the stamps before switching colors. Don't wear the shirts till they're dry!

Toothbrush Holders

Small clay flower pots make perfect sinkside stands! Supply each guest with a flower pot. Then use acrylic paints, paintbrushes, stencils, and sponge stamps to decorate your pots. Let the paint dry overnight.

Sleeping Bag Zipper Pulls

Use colorful beads and pieces of thin leather cord to make snazzy zipper pulls. Just knot one end of the cord, string a few beads onto it, slip it through the sleeping bag zipper tab, and knot the end. Make them for your backpacks, too!

Autograph Pillowcases

You'll need one white pillowcase for each guest, and a supply of fabric markers. On one side of your pillowcases, draw night scenes and write messages to one another, such as "When the day ends, we'll still be friends!" On the other side, draw morning scenes and write messages such as "I'll always care, even when you have morning hair!"

Friendship Rings

Twist up a bunch of colorful bead rings to share and wear.

You will need:
- An assortment of tiny "seed" beads
- Wire twist ties
- Scissors

1 Peel all the paper or plastic off a twist tie.

2 String beads onto the wire until the string is long enough to wrap around your finger.

3 Wrap the wire around your finger and twist the ends together to make a ring.

When the day ends, we'll still be friends!

I'll always care, even when you have morning hair!

Lights Out

When the lights go out, the fun's just begun!
Flashlight festivities make nighttime a bright time.

Out in a Wink

First, put slips of paper—one per guest—into a pillowcase. One slip should have an *X* on it. Have everyone pick a slip without showing it to anybody. The girl who picks the *X* is the Secret Winker. Have all the players sit in a circle with their flashlights under their faces. The Winker should then try to wink at someone without anyone else seeing. The winked-at player must turn her flashlight off and not say anything. The remaining players must try to figure out who the Winker is, while the Winker tries to "wink out" as many people as possible before being discovered.

Burglar Alarm

You'll need a windup alarm clock or timer that you can hear ticking in the dark. Set the alarm to go off a few minutes after you begin playing. Have everyone leave the room except one girl, who stays behind to hide the clock and turn off the lights. Have the group return to the room and, using only one flashlight, try to find the clock before—bzzzzzzz, time's up!

Flashlight Hide-and-Seek

Choose one girl to be It. Have her stand in the middle of the room with a flashlight and close her eyes. Then turn out the lights and have everyone hide. Each player must leave one part of her body showing. Then instruct It to point her flashlight in any direction and turn it on. If she sees someone, that person is out. She should continue to search in this way, always turning her flashlight off before moving it to another spot. The last player found is the winner.

Flashlight Basics

All you need is your imagination!

In the Spotlight
Set your flashlights up like spotlights on a stage. Take turns dancing, singing, or lip-synching to songs.

Silent Movies
Put on silent skits. Have the girls in the audience quickly click their flashlights off and on to give the effect of a flickering movie screen.

Flashlight Codes
Make up signals to flash in the dark. For example, use three quick blinks to mean "Please pass the popcorn!"

Shadow Puppets
Get everyone giggling and wiggling their hands. See who can create the scariest or silliest shape on the wall.

Party Tip

Have extra batteries on hand so your flashlights last as long as you do!

Psssst . . .

Crawl into your bags, turn off the lights, and whisper your secrets into the night!

What If

Think of fun questions to ask one another, such as "What would you do with a million dollars?" or "What if you could make yourself invisible?" Have each guest write one question on an index card, with three possible answers on the back. Put the cards into a pillowcase. Take turns drawing a card and reading the question and possible answers aloud. The girl reading the card should write down her answer. Everyone else should try to guess what she wrote. Each girl who guesses correctly gets a point. The girl with the most points after all the cards have been read wins.

What would you do if you won a million dollars?
a. give to homeless
b. buy horses
c. go to Disneyworld

Soooo Embarrassed!

Have each guest write her funniest memory or most embarrassing moment on a piece of paper and put it into a pillowcase. Then take turns drawing the pieces of paper from the pillowcase and reading the stories out loud.

Have every guest rate each story from 1 to 10, with 10 being the funniest or most embarrassing. Then add up the points and award a prize to the person with the winning story—if she'll admit it's hers!

Flashlight Circle Story

Have everyone sit in a circle. Have one girl hold a flashlight under her face and start telling a made-up story about herself and the girl next to her. After she has said a few sentences, she should turn off her flashlight. The next girl should then turn on her flashlight and continue the story, bringing the girl next to her into it. Keep passing the story along in this way until you've gone around the circle. The last girl must think of a way to end the story!

Need some ideas? Try one of these story starters:

(**Friend's name**) and I were riding our bikes the other day when suddenly the weather changed. The temperature dropped to freezing, the sky turned a purplish-green, and the wind began to howl. The next thing we knew . . .

One day, (**friend's name**) and I were walking home from school when suddenly we heard a strange gurgling noise. It was coming from a mailbox . . .

The field trip to the museum began like any other. But by the end of the day, (**friend's name**) and I had been through the most frightening experience of our life. It all began when we got lost in the dinosaur exhibit . . .

Party Tip

Try arranging your sleeping bags in different patterns. For example, form a star by putting all your heads in the middle. When someone wants to sleep, she can just turn her bag around the other way.

Rise & Shine

Breakfast Parfaits

Offer your guests a variety of yogurt flavors, cut-up fruit, and granola or other cereal to layer in pretty parfait glasses or tall drinking glasses.

Waffle Sandwiches

Toast up a stack of frozen waffles. Then serve them with a variety of spreads and toppings, such as:

- Peanut butter
- Applesauce
- Jelly
- Cinnamon sugar
- Sliced banana
- Cream cheese mixed with chopped apples, walnuts, and raisins

Strawberry-Cheesecake Burritos

Spread soft cream cheese and a thin layer of strawberry jam on flour tortillas. Crumble graham crackers on top, roll up, and eat!

Start the day in a delicious way! Wake up your guests with one of these scrumptious breakfasts.

You will find a big surprise in a small place.

Night-Before Breakfasts

Make your breakfasts before you go to bed, and you'll all have sweet dreams of tasty treats to come!

Frozen Yogurt Pops

You'll need one yogurt cup for each guest. If it's the kind with fruit on the bottom, be sure to stir it well. Then cover the tops with foil and poke popsicle sticks or plastic spoons through the top. Freeze overnight. In the morning, remove the popsicles from the containers by holding them under warm water for a few seconds and twisting the popsicles out.

Sleepy Bags

Have each guest decorate a paper lunch bag to look like her own sleeping bag. Then have each girl choose from an assortment of muffins, fruit, little cereal boxes, hard-boiled eggs, and juice to pack in her bag. In the morning, just grab your bags from the refrigerator and go back to the party room for breakfast in bed!

Fortune Napkins

For each guest, write a fun "fortune for today" on a paper napkin. Roll up a set of silverware in it, and tie it with a big, sunny bow.

Super Send-offs

You hold the Key to my heart.

Let's stick together.

Friendly Favors

Create clever favors that really say what you mean! Write a short-but-sweet message on a piece of paper and tape or tie it to a favor that goes with it.

Barrettes and Bands

Pass out scrunchies, clips, headbands, and other hair supplies as party favors to help that morning hair!

Souvenir Recording

Use a tape recorder to interview your pals while they pack their bags. Have them describe their favorite memories from the night before.

Who says the fun is over once the sun has come up? Plan a morning of silly surprises and special good-bye gifts.

Secret Notes

While your guests are eating breakfast, hide notes in their overnight bags. This will give your friends a fun surprise later when they unpack!

Sleepover Awards

Have an awards ceremony at breakfast. Give awards in humorous categories such as "Greatest Giggle," "Soundest Sleeper," and "Midnight Maniac." Hand out travel-size samples of toothpaste, shampoo, bubble bath, and hand lotion for fun prizes.

Dream Up a Theme

Give your sleepover an extra-special theme, and throw the slumber party of your dreams!

Island Party

Spend the night at my island getaway!
Where: Sophie's house 106 Pond Road
When: Friday, May 5,
Checkout time: 9:0[ ]
Make reservat[ ] by calling 55[ ]

To: Jennifer Garcia
222 West St.
[ ], NY 14627

Invitation to Paradise

For each guest, make a postcard by cutting tropical pictures out of travel magazines or brochures and gluing them to the front of an index card. On the back of the card, draw a line down the middle. Write information about the party on the left side, and the guest's address on the right. Add a stamp and mail it!

Sleep on the Beach

Transform your party room into your own private island. Spread out beach towels, set up beach chairs or lawn furniture, and open up beach umbrellas. Hang posters of tropical vacations—you can often get these for free at travel agencies. Cover tables with seashells and big crepe-paper flowers, available at most craft stores, or fill glass bowls with water and float real flower blossoms in them. Blow up beach balls for guests to play with, and play reggae, calypso, or other island music in the background.

Sip fruity drinks and hula the night away at your own tropical resort.

Warm Welcome

When your guests arrive, greet them the Hawaiian way by hanging a *lei,* or flower necklace, around their necks. You can buy plastic leis at most party supply stores. Or you can make your own paper leis by scrunching up balls of tissue paper and stringing them together with a needle and thread.

Cool Shades

Kick off the party by passing out inexpensive plastic sunglasses as favors. You and your guests can wear them all night long!

Hula Hoopla

Play Follow the Hula Leader! Take turns making up goofy hula dances for one another to try to follow.

Homemade Hula Skirts

Make your own grass skirts, then swish and sway away!

You will need:
- 1–2 rolls of green crepe paper
- Scissors
- Stapler or clear tape

1 To make the waistband, cut a piece of crepe paper long enough to go loosely around your waist.

2 Cut another strip about 2 feet long. Staple or tape it to one end of the waistband so that the strip hangs down straight. Cut another strip the same length and attach it right next to the first one. Keep going until you get to the end of the waistband.

3 Help each other wrap the finished skirts around your waists and staple or tape the ends together.

Island Buffet

Serve a taste of the tropics!

Ocean Motion

Serve tuna salad on a sea of lettuce. Or have an adult help you make a pineapple "boat" by slicing a pineapple in half, cutting out the inside, and filling the boat with tuna or chicken salad.

Floating Island Sundaes

For each guest, pour chocolate sauce into a bowl and gently drop a scoop of ice cream into it. Sprinkle the chocolate sauce with shredded coconut to look like foamy waves. Stick a pretty paper "beach" umbrella into the ice cream.

Fruit-Tasting Tray

Look for unusual tropical fruits such as mangoes, kiwis, pomegranates, star fruit, and papayas at the grocery store. Cut the fruit into pieces for your guests to sample.

"Fishy" Snacks

Fill a clean fishbowl with goldfish-shaped crackers.

Caribbean Breeze

With an adult's help, fill a blender about ⅓ full with ice. Then add 2 cups of pineapple juice, 1 cup of orange juice, and half a banana. Blend until smooth.

Strawberry Sunrise

Break an 8-ounce package of frozen strawberries into pieces small enough to go in the blender. Add 2 cups of 7-Up or Sprite. With an adult's help, blend until smooth.

Island Anklets

Supply your guests with a variety of beads and thin leather cord to make ankle bracelets. Each of you should cut a piece of cord long enough to wrap around your ankle twice, then tie a knot at one end of the cord. String beads onto the cord until the string is almost long enough to wrap around your ankle. Tie a knot after the last bead, and tie your bracelet around your ankle. Trim off any extra cord.

Flashlight Limbo

Turn off the lights and have one person shine a flashlight straight out, about three feet off the floor. Have everyone else take turns "limboing" under the beam. Each player must pass under it without ducking forward or touching the floor with her hands or knees. If any part of her body crosses through the light, she's out. Lower the beam after everyone has had a turn. How low can you go?

Tidal Wave

You'll need a ball of socks for each player, and a bed sheet. Have everyone stand around the sheet and toss her socks into the middle. Then everyone should grab the edges of the sheet, lift it up, and try to bounce each other's socks off by shaking and waving the sheet. The girl whose socks stay on the longest wins.

Carnival Fun Night

Step right up! Invite your friends to an exciting night of games, prizes, and mouthwatering delights.

Enter Here

Turn your party room into a festive midway! Use brightly colored streamers, balloons, and holiday lights to create a crazy carnival scene. Hang colorful signs on the wall directing your guests to different places, such as the concession stand and the photo booth.

KAREN'S CARNIVAL

FOOD →

← PHOTO BOOTH

FACE PAINTING →

Free Admission

For each guest, cut a ticket shape out of construction paper. On the front of the ticket write "Admit One." Make up a different three-digit number for each ticket and write the number on both ends of the ticket. On the back write information about the party. Instruct your guests to bring their tickets to the party for a special drawing.

Win a Goldfish!

When each guest arrives, take her ticket and tear it in half. Put one half in a bowl and give the other half back. After everyone has arrived, draw one ticket stub. The girl with the matching number is the lucky winner—of a real goldfish! They're available at most pet stores. Keep the fish in a bowl overnight, then let the winner take it home in a plastic bag filled with water.

Gum-Ball Guess

Fill a jar with gum balls. Then invite everyone to guess how many gum balls are in the jar. Have each guest write down her guess. Pour out the gum balls and count them. The girl whose guess is closest to the actual number wins a prize. Then share the gum balls with the group and have a bubble-blowing contest!

Face Painting

Use face paints, available at most costume or hobby shops, to create hearts, flowers, stars, and kooky clown faces on one another's cheeks. You can also use lipstick and eye liner. Have tissues and cold cream or makeup remover on hand to wipe off the paints when you're through.

Basket Toss

Use five buckets or large pots as "baskets." Set them up one behind the other in a straight line. Put small prizes or pieces of candy in each one. Create a starting line in front of the first basket. Then invite each player to stand at the line and try to toss a beanbag or soft ball into the first basket. If she misses, her turn is over. If she makes the basket, she gets to take a prize from it and take another turn, aiming for the second basket, and so on.

Concession Stand

Set out these traditional carnival snacks on a special table decorated with streamers and balloons. Hang a sign near the table, listing everything available at the stand.

Cheese Fries
Snow Cones
Carnival Corn

Cheese Fries

Cook frozen French fries and serve them in paper cups—dripping with cheese sauce! For the sauce, combine ¼ cup of milk and 1 pound of Velveeta, cut into small cubes, in a microwave-safe bowl. Microwave on HIGH for 1½ minutes, then stir. Microwave for another 1 to 2 minutes, stirring every 30 seconds until smooth.

Snow Cones

Fill a blender halfway with ice cubes. Have an adult help you blend the ice into small pieces, then scoop into paper cups. Invite your guests to choose from a variety of fruit juices and punch to pour over the ice.

Carnival Corn

For each guest, roll a piece of construction paper into a cone. Use tape to fasten the sides. Then fill the cone with popcorn. Offer your guests a choice of plain, cheddar-flavored, or caramel corn!

Dogs-on-a-Stick

Each of you can make your own piping-hot pup.

You will need:

- Cooked hot dogs, 1 for each guest
- Wooden sticks, 1 for each hot dog
- Tube of ready-made crescent dough, such as Pillsbury
- Baking sheet
- Mustard, ketchup, and relish

1 Insert a wooden stick into one end of each hot dog.

2 Separate the dough into triangles. Place each hot dog on its side on a triangle, along the bottom edge. Roll the dough around the hot dog.

3 Have an adult help you place the hot dogs on a baking sheet and cook according to the directions for the dough. Serve with mustard, ketchup, and relish.

Bowl 'em Over!

You'll need to collect ten 2-liter plastic soda bottles ahead of time. Fill the bottles with about two inches of water to weigh them down, and screw on the caps tightly. Then, in an open space, set the bottles up like bowling pins. They should form a triangle pointing toward you—one pin in front, a row of two behind it, then a row of three, then four. Determine a starting line a few feet from the pins. Take turns standing at the line and trying to knock over the pins by rolling a tennis ball at them. Give each girl two tries. Keep track of how many pins each player knocks down. See who scores the most!

Photo Booth

Set aside a corner of the room where you and your guests can take turns having your picture taken. For especially silly snapshots, provide dress-up clothes, hats, and masks to pose in. After the party, have the film developed and give each girl a copy of her picture as a souvenir.

Party Tip

Need some ideas for inexpensive prizes? Try lollipops, miniature candy bars, stickers, magnets, pencils, and plastic beads. For bigger prizes, give out small stuffed animals, yo-yos, jacks, playing cards, and other little toys.

Camp-In

Create your own starry sky and cozy campsite, then invite your friends to camp in with you!

At-TENT-ion!

Pitch the party to your friends by passing out tent-shaped invitations.

You will need:
- 8½-by-11-inch sheets of paper, 1 for each guest
- Pen
- Scissors
- Hole punch
- Thin ribbon or yarn

1 Lay the paper sideways on a table or flat surface. Fold the 2 top corners down to meet in the middle. Cut off the bottom of the paper along the base of the triangle.

2 Open the flaps and write the information about the party inside. Remind your guests to bring their "camping gear"—a sleeping bag, a flashlight, and a water bottle or canteen.

3 Punch a hole in each tent flap. Thread a piece of yarn or ribbon through the holes, and tie in a bow.

Setting Up Camp

Convert your party room into a comfortable campground.

Cut moon and star shapes out of poster board, then cover them with tin foil. Have an adult help you use thread and clear tape to hang them from the ceiling.

Place teddy bears and other stuffed animals around the room to create "wildlife."

Use a cooler to store drinks and snacks for on-the-spot refreshment.

Pitch a tent! Tie a piece of rope between two chairs, then drape a sheet over it. Pull the sides of the sheet out and weigh them down with books or other heavy objects.

Mess Kits

For each guest, wrap a napkin, plastic silverware, a prepackaged wet wipe, and a bag of gummy bears or gummy worms in a bandanna. Tie closed with a ribbon.

Creepy-Crawly Napkins

Decorate paper napkins with little black ants! Use a pencil eraser and an ink pad to stamp three dots in a row for each ant's body. Use a black felt-tip pen to draw on legs and antennae.

Food for Hungry Hikers

Spread out a picnic blanket and enjoy some good grub!

Trail Mix

Set out bowls of granola, nuts, chocolate chips, raisins, and other dried fruit. Give each guest a small plastic bag and have her mix up her own combo.

Wiener Roast

Serve hot dogs with a variety of toppings, such as shredded cheese, chili, onions, and pickle relish.

Bug Juice

Fill a big thermos with lemonade. Have your guests fill up their water bottles or canteens to sip from all night long.

Stacks of S'mores

 Set out graham crackers, marshmallows, chocolate bars, sliced bananas, peanut butter, and different jams. Combine them any way you want! Stack the fillings on a graham cracker with the marshmallow last. Put on a plate and microwave on **HIGH** for 15 to 20 seconds, or until the marshmallow puffs up. Add the top cracker and press down. Let cool before eating.

Nature Treasure Hunt

Hide bunches of dried flowers, twigs, leaves, and pinecones around the house. Tie a note to each treasure, giving a clue to where the next one is hidden. Invite your guests to go on a hike looking for them. When all the items have been found, use them to make picture frames. Cut frames out of cardboard, and glue the dried petals, leaves, and other bits to the frames.

Mosquito Bite

You can play this game throughout the night. Give each girl a sheet of colored dot stickers. The idea is to get rid of all your dots by sticking them onto other girls without getting caught. But be careful—if you get caught leaving a "bite" on someone, she gets to leave a bite on you instead!

Pom-Pom Critters

Make cuddly woodland creatures out of yarn and felt.

You will need:
- 3 or 4 balls of different colored yarns
- Ruler
- Scissors
- Scraps of felt
- Glue

1 Cut a piece of yarn about 4 inches long and set it aside.

2 Tie the end of the ball of yarn loosely around 2 of your fingers. Then wrap the yarn around those fingers 50 to 75 times. The more times you wrap it, the fluffier your pom-pom will be.

3 Carefully slide the yarn off your fingers and pinch it together in the middle to make a bow shape. Tie the short piece of yarn tightly around the middle.

4 Cut through all the loops with scissors. Shape the yarn into a ball by fluffing and trimming the ends with scissors.

5 Glue little pieces of felt to your pom-poms to make faces, ears, and tiny feet.

Campfire Favorites

Stack your flashlights in a pile to make a glowing fire. Then gather around and play these silly circle games.

Weird Wildlife Sounds

Have each girl write on a slip of paper the name of an unusual animal. Put the slips into a pillowcase. Take turns drawing a slip, imitating or making up the sound of the animal you picked, and challenging the others to guess the animal. See how long it takes for everyone to stop laughing and start guessing!

Mirror, Mirror

Have one girl make a goofy face at the girl sitting next to her. That girl must then make the same face at the girl sitting next to her, and so on, going all the way around the circle. See how far you can get without giggling, and see how much the face has changed by the time it's back to the girl who started it!

Follow the Ranger

Choose one girl to be It. Have her leave the room while the rest of you pick someone to be the "Ranger." The Ranger should start doing an action, such as snapping her fingers or wiggling her nose. The rest of you must follow the action. Have It come back into the room and stand in the middle of the circle. The Ranger should change actions as the group follows along and It tries to guess who the Ranger is. If It guesses correctly, the Ranger becomes It. If she does not guess correctly after three tries, she's out.

Mystery and

There's magic in the air! Invite your friends to join you for an enchanted evening of fortune-telling and surprises.

I see a slumber party in your future.
    Color below to reveal your destiny.
Place: Madame Liza's house
    64 Hill Blvd.
Date: Sat., Oct. 18
Time: 6:00 P.M.
Pickup at 8:30 A.M. Sunday

Invisible Invitations

For each guest you'll need a sheet of white paper, a rubber band, and a highlighter pen—any color except yellow. At the top of the paper, use a regular marker or pen to write a mysterious message telling your guest to color over the invitation with the highlighter. Then use a white crayon to write the information about the party. Wrap the note around the highlighter and secure with a rubber band.

Secret Sleepover Den

Create a special entrance by hanging long strands of beads in the doorway. Or hang wind chimes that tinkle whenever someone passes by. Throughout the room, spread out big cushions and pillows to lounge on. Drape exotic-looking scarves or pieces of material over the furniture and windows. Dim the lights and, with a parent's permission, burn incense or scented candles.

Tangled Web

You'll need a ball of yarn for each guest. Use the same color for everyone if you want to give your guests a real challenge! Tie the loose end of each ball around a party favor, then tuck the favor into a small hiding place somewhere in the room. Unwind each ball of yarn, weaving it over, under, and around objects in the room. At the end of the unwrapped yarn, tie or tape a slip of paper with a guest's name on it. When your guests arrive, have them "untangle the mystery" and follow their yarn to a special surprise!

Magic Night

"You Are Getting Hungry..."

Bewitch your guests with tricky treats, wizard's sweets, and a frothy, foaming brew!

Mystery Meals

Make a variety of sandwiches, such as turkey, cheese, and peanut butter and jelly. Wrap each sandwich and pack it in a shoebox with a piece of fruit. Sprinkle confetti stars and moons in each box, and tuck in a small favor. Wrap the boxes, then invite each guest to choose one. Have some extra sandwiches and fruit on hand in case a guest doesn't like what she gets.

Question-Mark Cupcakes

Use your favorite cake mix to bake cupcakes. Make a question mark on top of each one with frosting.

Luck of the Draw

Set out a big bowl of fortune cookies for your guests. You can buy fortune cookies at most grocery stores.

Foaming Magic Brew

Scoop vanilla ice cream—one scoop per guest—into a large bowl or punch bowl. Pour root beer over the ice cream until the ice cream is covered. Then ladle the foaming brew into glasses, and serve with a straw and a spoon.

Wizard Sticks

These crunchy snacks are sure to cast a spell over everyone!

You will need:
- 1 cup white chocolate chips
- Microwave-safe bowl
- Pretzel rods
- Tall plastic cup
- A variety of sprinkles or candy silver balls
- Wax paper

1 With an adult, microwave the chocolate chips on MEDIUM HIGH for 1 minute. Remove and stir. Continue microwaving for 30 seconds at a time, stirring in between, until smooth.

2 Pour the chocolate into the cup. Dip a pretzel into the chocolate, tilting the cup and turning the rod to coat it evenly with a thin layer of chocolate. Let the excess drip off the end of the pretzel.

3 Gently shake the sprinkles over the dipped pretzel, then set on wax paper to cool. Let the chocolate harden for 1 hour before eating.

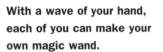

Poof!

With a wave of your hand, each of you can make your own magic wand.

You will need:
- Cardboard tubes from coat hangers, one for each guest
- Aluminum foil
- Construction paper
- Pencil and ruler
- Scissors and glue
- Glitter
- Ribbon

1 Cover each tube with aluminum foil.

2 For each wand, stack 2 pieces of construction paper together and draw a star about 4 inches wide on the top sheet. Cut out the star, cutting through both sheets.

3 Glue 1 star to the end of the tube, about 1 inch down. Then glue the other star to the same end of the tube on the facing side so that the stars' edges match up.

4 Decorate the wand with glitter. Let dry. Then tie long streams of ribbon to the wand, just below the stars.

Blue Clue

Keep your friends guessing with this sneaky trick. Ask the group for a volunteer. Take the volunteer out of the room and explain to her that you will be going back into the room alone to ask the group to pick an object. Explain that you will then call her back in and point to various objects around the room, asking which one is the chosen object. Tell her that the correct object will be the one you point to right after you point to something that is blue. When she identifies the chosen object, everyone will think she has magical powers!

That's it!

Disappearing Objects

Collect several small objects, such as a marble, a button, a bead, an earring, a penny, a paper clip, a thimble, and a pair of dice. Put the objects in a hat and give your guests one minute to study the objects carefully. Then choose a girl to hold a scarf in front of you while you remove an object and hide it from view. Don't let the scarf holder peek! Then let everyone look again. Each girl should write down the object she thinks is missing. If she's right, she gets a point. Give everyone a turn as the object remover. Then add up the points to see who is the super sleuth!

Anna, you will be a dentist living in Indiana married to a famous movie star. Your hobby will be skydiving.

Favorite hobby

Who lives with you

Name

Career

Where you live

Funny Fortunes

You'll need five paper bags. Write *Name* on one bag. On each of the other bags, write a different category, such as *Career, Where you live, Who lives with you*, and *Favorite hobby*. Pass out small pieces of paper or index cards. Have each girl write her name on a card and put it into the *Name* bag. Then have everyone write something silly or serious to put in each of the other bags. Line up the bags, with the *Name* bag first. Take turns being the fortune-teller by drawing a name, drawing a card out of each of the other bags, and telling what the future holds for that person.

Dice Advice

On a sheet of paper, list the numbers 1 to 12. Next to each number write a word or phrase that could answer any question, such as "definitely," "dream on," or "roll again." Then take turns asking a yes-or-no question, such as "Will I be famous when I grow up?" Roll a pair of dice and look up the number you rolled on the sheet to learn the answer to your question.

All-in-One Celebration

Happy Fourth of Hallowthanksmastine's Eve-ster!
Get in the holiday spirit at a party that celebrates them all.

Holiday Puzzle

Create a word search using the names of all your favorite holidays. Then invite your friends to celebrate these holidays in one exciting night.

You will need:
- Graph paper
- Pencil and markers
- Construction paper
- Glue

1 Draw a big square on graph paper. Inside it write the name of each holiday—1 letter per box—going across or down. Fill in the leftover boxes with other letters to complete the square.

2 Hand-copy or photocopy the puzzle as many times as there are guests.

3 For each guest, fold a sheet of construction paper in half and glue the puzzle to the front.

4 Below the puzzle, instruct your guests to look for the holidays you've listed and to come to a party celebrating them.

5 On the inside of the card, give information about the party. Instruct your guests to bring a small wrapped present for a holiday gift exchange.

Find the holidays in the puzzle, then come celebrate them all!

Halloween   Valentine's Day
Thanksgiving   New Year's Eve
Christmas   Easter
Fourth of July

It's a 4th of Hallowthanksmastine's Eve-ster slumber party!

Where: Tamika's house

When: Friday, Feb. 5, 6:00

Pickup Time: 8:30 A.M. Saturday

Please bring a small wrapped present.

Holiday House

Mix up the seasons with decorations that range from spooky to sweet.

Seasonal Symbols

Cut out an assortment of holiday shapes such as Valentine hearts, Thanksgiving turkeys, and Halloween pumpkins from construction paper. Tape the shapes to the walls.

Stocking Stuffers

Hang Christmas stockings, one for each guest, along the edge of a table, windowsill, or mantelpiece. Fill with candy or small favors, and label each stocking with a guest's name. When your guests arrive, put the gifts they bring in a large pillowcase near the stockings to open in the morning.

Haunting Touches

Hang creepy Halloween decorations, such as fake spiderwebs and rubber bats, from the ceiling.

Stars and Stripes

Hang red, white, and blue streamers and blow up bunches of red, white, and blue balloons. Buy or make small paper flags for your guests to wave throughout the night.

Happy New Year!

Fill the room with alarm clocks set to go off at midnight.

Scrumptious Supper

Serve up a feast of your favorite holiday foods.

Creamy Winter Nog

Have an adult help you mix 3 big scoops of vanilla ice cream, ½ cup milk, ½ teaspoon nutmeg, and ½ teaspoon cinnamon in a blender. Blend until smooth. Serve with a cinnamon candy cane for dipping and licking!

Holiday Cookies

Use ready-made sugar cookie dough, cookie cutters, and cookie decorations to make Valentine's Day hearts, Fourth of July stars, Halloween pumpkins, and other shapes.

Thanksgiving Turkey Sandwiches

Set out sliced turkey, bread or rolls, lettuce, mayonnaise, cranberry sauce, and stuffing made from a mix or from scratch. Invite your guests to build turkey dinners on a bun!

Caramel Apples

These traditional Halloween treats are juicy and sweet!

You will need:
- An apple for each guest
- Wooden sticks, 1 for each apple
- A bag of caramels (makes 4 or 5 apples)
- Microwave-safe bowl
- Mixing spoon
- 2 tablespoons water
- Optional toppings, such as chopped nuts or shredded coconut
- Wax paper greased with butter or shortening

1 Wash the apples and twist off the stems. Insert a stick into each apple where the stem was.

2 Unwrap the caramels and put them in the bowl. Add the water. Have an adult help you microwave on HIGH for 2½ to 3½ minutes, stirring every minute, until smooth.

3 Dip the apples in the caramel. Turn to coat evenly. Scrape off the bottoms to remove any extra caramel.

4 Roll the apples in the toppings of your choice, then stand the apples up on the wax paper. Let cool for 15 minutes before eating.

Firecracker Popcorn

Melt 1 tablespoon of margarine or butter. Then stir in ¾ teaspoon taco seasoning and about ¾ teaspoon Tabasco sauce. Combine the mixture in a plastic bag with 5 cups of popped popcorn. Close the bag tightly and shake to coat evenly.

Easter Egg Art

Why wait for the Easter Bunny to decorate eggs?

You will need:

- Food coloring
- White vinegar, 1 teaspoon per color
- Plastic cups, 1 per color
- Newspaper and paper towels
- Spoons, 1 for each guest
- About 1 dozen hard-boiled eggs
- Permanent markers and stickers

1 Have an adult help you make different colors of dye. For each color, mix ½ cup boiling water, ½ teaspoon food coloring, and 1 teaspoon vinegar in a plastic cup.

2 Cover your work area with newspaper. Use spoons to place your eggs into the dye. Wait for the eggs to turn the shade you want, then remove them from the dye and lay them on a paper towel to dry for about 30 minutes.

3 When the eggs have dried, decorate them with permanent markers and stickers.

Trim the Turkey

On a large piece of paper, draw the shape of a turkey's head and body. Hang the drawing on the wall. Then cut out feet, tail feathers, a beak, and a wattle (the flap that hangs from the neck) from construction paper. Give a turkey part and a piece of tape to each guest. Blindfold the first girl, spin her around three times, and have her try to tape her turkey part to the right place on the drawing. Give everyone a turn. The girl who gets her part closest to the right spot wins.

Trick or Treat Scavenger Hunt

Hide bowls of bite-size candy around the house. Place a note in each bowl, giving a clue to where the next bowl is hidden. Then provide your guests with "trick or treat" bags and a clue to where the first bowl is hidden. Invite your guests to take a piece of candy from each bowl as they find it.

Clue #1: There's something fishy about where this bowl is hidden.

Be My Valentine

Provide everyone with pink and red construction paper, paper doilies, stickers, glitter, glue, scissors, and markers. Then make Valentine cards for each other, with silly or sweet messages written on them. Throughout the night, sneak the Valentines into each other's belongings—in sleeping bags, under pillows, or anywhere else they'll be discovered later.

Countdown to Midnight

When the clock strikes 12, it's time to ring in the New Year! A few minutes before midnight, pass out confetti, noisemakers, and hats. Fill plastic champagne glasses with sparkling juice or ginger ale. Then count down to the big moment and celebrate!

Merry Morning!

In the morning, give each girl her Christmas stocking and have her pick a present out of the grab-bag pillowcase you filled the night before.

Party Tip

Collect holiday decorations and candy throughout the year. They're often on sale right after the holiday, and they're hard to find at other times of the year.

Star-Studded Sleepover

Plan a glamorous evening of Hollywood-style dining and celebrating.

Guest Stars

For each guest, draw a star on poster board and cut it out. Then use a hole punch to punch holes all the way around the star, about ¼ inch from the edge. Weave thin silver or gold ribbon through the holes, and tie a bow at the top of the star. Use a silver or gold pen to write the party information on the star. Remind your guests to wear their party best!

You're invited to the celebrity event of the season. Dress formal.

Where: The V.I.P. Room (Lee's house) 201 Third Ave.
When: Friday, July 9 7:00 P.M.
Pickup at 9:30 A.M. Saturday

V.I.P. Room

Give your guests the red-carpet treatment! Roll out a long piece of red cloth leading up to the door of the party room. Cut a star shape out of cardboard, write "V.I.P.s only" on it, and hang it on the door. Blow up bunches of black, white, silver, and gold balloons to give the room a festive lift. Put cutout magazine photos of famous people in picture frames, and place them around the room.

The Lead Role

Write the names of favorite movie or TV stars on slips of paper and put them into a pillowcase. Then have each guest draw a name. For the rest of the night, pretend to be whomever you picked. Call each other by your star names!

Dominique, dah-ling, you look mah-velous!

Photograph Relay

You'll need two suitcases or duffel bags, each packed with glamorous dress-up clothing, lipstick, blush, eye shadow, and a disposable camera. Divide the group into two teams. Give each team a suitcase. At the word *go,* one player from each team must open her team's suitcase, put on the clothes, have her teammates do her makeup, then strike a pose for the camera! The first team to photograph all of its players in this way wins. After the party, have the photos developed and give each guest her "glamour" picture.

Magazine Scavenger Hunt

Divide your guests into two teams. Give each team a stack of old magazines and a list of items to find in them, such as beauty products, different kinds of clothing, or specific celebrities. The teams should tear out the photos as they find them. The first team to find all the items wins.

Pajama Fashion Show

Have each girl write on an index card a silly description of her sleep outfit, pointing out its details and special features. Then have each guest walk down the "runway" modeling her sleepwear while someone else acts as the announcer and reads the humorous description.

Dazzling Dinner Table

Dress up your table with a fancy cloth, candlesticks, and confetti sprinkled around the center. Then treat your guests to an elegant meal.

Simple Starters

Pass around *hors d'oeuvres*, or appetizers, such as celery sticks with cream cheese, mini pizza rolls, or other bite-size delicacies from the frozen foods section of your grocery store.

Flowery Favors

Place dried flowers in miniature vases or glass bottles decorated with ribbon. Put one at each setting. Let your guests keep the vases as party favors.

Place Cards

Put a name card at each setting to show your guests where to sit.

Pastry Tray

Line a plate with paper doilies. Arrange pretty cookies, brownies, and other sweet treats on the plate.

Finger Bowls

Give each guest a small bowl of water with a thin lemon slice in it, to dip her fingers into when she's finished eating.

Fancy Folded Napkins

Turn a napkin into a tuxedo jacket with a few simple folds.

1 Completely unfold a cloth or paper napkin. Then fold it diagonally to make a triangle.

2 Fold the creased edge over about 1 inch.

3 Turn the napkin over and fold the 2 corners down to meet at the point of the triangle.

4 Turn the napkin over again and fold the 2 side corners into the middle so the tips touch. Fold the bottom point into the middle.

5 Turn the finished jacket over. Use ribbon to tie a bow around a knife, fork, and spoon. Tuck the utensils inside the jacket, and slide the ribbon up toward the neck to make a bow tie.

Star Sandwiches
Use soft bread and fillings such as cheese, peanut butter and jelly, or cold cuts to make a variety of sandwiches. Cut stars out of the middles with a star-shaped cookie cutter.

Pretty Punch
In a big punch bowl, mix equal amounts of orange juice and 7-Up or Sprite. Add ice cubes and 3 big scoops of rainbow sherbet. Serve the punch in plastic champagne glasses.

Friendship Star-Walk

Invite your guests to leave their mark of friendship on your own version of the Hollywood Walk of Fame.

You will need:

- Construction paper
- Scissors and glue
- Pens or markers
- A 6-foot-long sheet of butcher paper, or 2 large pieces of poster board taped together
- Newspaper
- Smocks or old shirts
- Finger paints
- Paper plates

1 Have each guest cut a large star shape out of construction paper and write her signature and the date on it.

2 Glue all the stars onto the butcher paper or poster board, spaced evenly apart in a row. Leave enough space under each star to fit a pair of handprints.

3 Spread newspaper over your work area. Put on your smocks or old shirts. Pour some finger paint onto a paper plate, and spread it around with your fingers.

4 Have each girl press her hands into the paint and stamp on the sheet under her autographed star.

Sleepover Spa

Pamper yourselves after a busy evening of photo sessions and autograph parties! Supply curlers, ponytail holders, barrettes, nail polish, nail files, and other beauty supplies, and take turns doing one another's hair and nails.

Extra Frills

Fill a pillowcase with costume jewelry, hair accessories, and other beauty supplies to use throughout the night. In the morning, let each guest pull one item out of the bag without looking and keep it as a party favor.

Sleepover Memory Book

Good Night

Sleepover Memory Book

For a special souvenir of your party, make this mini memory book. Follow the directions on the next page to put the book together. Then fill in the details of your party. Before each guest leaves, have her complete a page by signing her name and writing her favorite memory of the party.

Food ....

Activities and Games ....

I stayed awake until .... o'clock!

My favorite moment ....

Friend

Name ....

I stayed awake until .... o'clock!

My favorite moment ....

Pal

Name ....

I stayed awake until .... o'clock!

My favorite moment ....

Chum

Name ....

I stayed awake until .... o'clock!

My favorite moment ....

1 Cut out each pair of pages only on the solid black lines. Be sure to cut around the tabs marked with the letters A, B, and C.

2 Stack the pages on top of one another in alphabetical order, as shown, with the letters on the tabs facing up.

3 Fold the stack of pages in half along the center lines. The cover of the book should now be on the top. Run your thumbnail down the folded edges to help the pages lie flat.

4 Open the folded stack. Staple along the center line. Cut off the tabs, and you're finished!

A Night to Remember

Whenever I want
to remember this night
And all the friends who
made it JUST RIGHT,
All I have to do is look
inside my Sleepover Memory Book!

My name ....

Date of party ....

Theme (if any) ....

Decorations ....

Buddy

Name ....

I stayed awake until .... o'clock!

My favorite moment ....

Friend

Name ....

I stayed awake until .... o'clock!

My favorite moment ....

Buddy

Name ....

I stayed awake until .... o'clock!

My favorite moment ....

Chum

Name ....

I stayed awake until .... o'clock!

My favorite moment ....

Pal

Name ....

I stayed awake until .... o'clock!

My favorite moment ....